BLACKBURN IN FOCUS

by

Alan Duckworth and Jim Halsall

Landy Publishing
2002

ISBN 1 872895 58 1
A catalogue record of this book is available from the British Library.
Layout by Mike Clarke. *Tel/Fax: 01254 395848*
Printed by Nayler the Printer Ltd., Accrington. *Tel: 01254 234247*

Landy Publishing have also published:

Blackburn in Times Gone By compiled by Jim Halsall
Blackburn Tram Rides by Jim Halsall
A Blackburn Childhood in Wartime by Marjorie Clayton
A Blackburn Miscellany edited by Bob Dobson
Blackburn & Darwen a Century Ago by Alan Duckworth
Accrington Observed by Brian Brindle and Bob Dobson
Accrington's Changing Face by Frank Watson and Bob Dobson
Accrington's Public Transport by Robert Rush
Bolland Forest & the Hodder Valley by Greenwood and Bolton

A full list is available from:

Landy Publishing
'Acorns' 3 Staining Rise, Staining, Blackpool, FY3 0BU
Tel/Fax: 01253 895678

INTRODUCTION

John William Shaw died in his 92nd year in September 1940. Right up until his 90th birthday he had been printing photographs without the aid of spectacles. He was born at East Harling in Norfolk. His father was an agricultural worker and at the age of 8 John joined him, looking after livestock and being generally useful round the farm. In the 1860's his father took employment with Robert West, a farmer on the Feilden estate at Feniscowles. John had wanted to be a blacksmith for some time and became a tenant of a smithy in Simmons St.

Photography was an exciting new technology at the time. Shaw had already encountered it in Norfolk when a travelling photographer made his regular visits. He purchased the necessary equipment and was soon engaged in producing commercial postcards of local views. He also photographed groups of people, his very first such being of St Mary's School in Mellor.

Shaw had 3 sons and a daughter. Two of his sons shared his interest in photography; Alfred eventually joining him in the business. Shaw lived for a time in Whalley New Rd., but by 1903 had premises in Preston New Rd from which father and son conducted their photography business. Towards the end of his life he lived with his son-in-law, J H A Swindlehurst, who was headmaster of Furthergate School.

Alfred Shaw started his working life in the cotton mills, before becoming a conductor on the horse drawn trams and later an inspector. He joined his father's business at the turn of the century, a venture which continued until the First World War when many of the firm's negatives which had been sent to Germany for colour printing were lost. Alfred persevered with postcard publishing after the war, before becoming manager of the billiard hall in Lord St and later an employee of John Chew and Co, with whom he stayed until 1950.

Alfred was a keen cyclist and no doubt roved the Ribble Valley and beyond looking for picturesque views. He had a love of local history and contributed many articles to the Blackburn Times and the Northern Daily Telegraph. His wife died in 1934. Alfred survived her by 20 years, dying on 28th of December 1954 at the age of 80.

The glass negatives produced by Shaw father and son came to Blackburn library and although prints of some of Blackburn's best known landmarks were made, the vast

John William Shaw, possibly taken by his son Alfred.

Alfred Shaw - a keen cyclist.

indicated by the detailed close ups that it has been possible to include. The Shaws were masters of their craft, there's no doubt about that; what there is some doubt about is who exactly was responsible for each of the photographs. Many of the photographs date from around 1910 - 12. By then J W Shaw was in his sixties, so perhaps it was A E who was out and about with the photographic equipment. So when we refer to Shaw throughout the book we are inclined to believe that it was A E behind the lens and J W in the dark room putting his years of experience to the task of developing and printing his son's efforts, but we cannot be sure.

Putting this book together has been a joint effort. Jim's local knowledge and photographic skills have, I hope, been complemented by my research and caption writing. We are indebted to Ken Hampshire for putting his vast knowledge of Blackburn and its people at our disposal and to the staff at Blackburn Library, Information Development Services Manager Ian Sutton and Community History Manager Diana Rushton for all their help, encouragement and advice. You can visit the library's website at www.blackburnworld.com.

Thanks also to Tom Lord of the Red Rose Picture Postcard Club and to Nick Harling of Blackburn Museum for the loan of some cartes-de-visite advertising the services of some Blackburn photographers who would be known to the Shaws.

Alan Duckworth
Blackburn Library
March 2002

majority were preserved in storage for many years. It was only in 2001 as a result of a chance conversation that Jim Halsall volunteered for the task of identifying and listing the collection.

It was immediately clear that this was not just a collection of local importance, not just of significance to Lancashire, but that the library had a collection of regional, if not national, importance. The Shaws had ranged far and wide; into Yorkshire, the Lake District, Derbyshire and beyond. Jim began cleaning and making prints. So impressed was he with their quality, that he experimented by *'zooming in'* on interesting features in the background. The results throw fascinating light on everyday life in Edwardian Blackburn. Jim became determined that a way should be found to allow as many people as possible to view the collection. Hence the publication of this book, which covers Blackburn and surrounding areas such as Pleasington, Wilpshire and Salesbury. It is hoped that further books based on Shaw's photographs will follow. An exhibition of Shaw's work is planned for next year at Blackburn Museum.

As you peruse these photographs, two things will be immediately clear: the artistry of the photographers, revealed in the composition of the shots, and the technical quality, as

Opposite: Two studio portraits of Alfred, possibly taken by his father.

WITTON STOCKS, Nr BLACKBURN.

This is a view from Witton Stocks looking towards Redlam and Blackburn. From January 26th, 1889, the horse drawn tram route came as far as the Griffin Inn at Redlam Brow. On March 11th, 1899, the new electrified route was extended to Witton Stocks and on October 10th, 1903, the line was extended yet again as far as Cherry Tree. This was the only route to have been twice extended. Note the pole of barber John Dodds on the right. Traditionally these were striped red and white.

A view along Preston Old Rd looking towards Witton Stocks. Cartmel Street is on the right and the land just before it became the site for Scapa, who started their business in 1927. It is now occupied by Voith Fabrics. Before the First World War there was a skating rink nearby on Cartmel Road. In the distance is St Philip's Church. Note the electric tram standards and the adjacent gas lamps. Note too that they are situated down one side of the street only.

In February 2002, Jim Halsall's photo shows the former Scapa premises on the right, now occupied by Voith Fabrics. Note traffic calming measures on right, otherwise the present day scene is remarkably similar to Shaw's version.

FENISCLIFFE BRIDGE, WITTON.

Another view of the River Darwen as it flows under Feniscliffe Bridge, just beyond the entrance to Witton Park on the Cherry Tree tram route. In 1931 the road and bridge were widened from 32 feet to 60 feet. A new reinforced concrete bridge replaced the stone one in the picture.

The River Darwen rises on the moors above Darwen at Cranberry Moss. The waters used to gather in Jack Key's Lodge, now a grassy depression where once there were boats for hire. The river continues through Sough to the centre of Darwen, though its appearances above ground are fleeting. At Blackburn it is joined by the Blakewater. It flows on to Hoghton and joins the Ribble at Walton-le-dale. This is an idyllic shot at Witton, but it was not long before the river's stench drove the Feildens from their home at Feniscowles Hall.

THE RIVER DARWEN, WITTON.

A shot of Feniscliffe Brow with the entrance to Witton Park on the right and a single deck tram at the crest of the hill. In the foreground at the left is the Feilden memorial and drinking fountain. This was erected in memory of Randle Francis Feilden who died of typhoid in 1886 at the age of 24. Only three years earlier lavish celebrations had taken place at Witton House for Randle's coming of age. The fountain was in disuse by 1910 and in 1931 when the road was widened the memorial was taken down.

FENISCOWLES VIADUCT.

This close-up shows the group under the gas lamp in remarkable detail. It looks like they have a long walk ahead of them down the road.

A rail link between Blackburn and Chorley was first suggested in the 1840s, but it wasn't until 1864, when Wigan coal mine owners saw the line as the best way to get coal to the expanding market in Blackburn, that the plan became a reality. Work was completed in 1869. The line cut the distance by rail between Blackburn and Chorley from 21 miles to a little over nine and, it was said, would cut the price of coal in Blackburn by one shilling a ton.

There's an autumnal atmosphere about this view of the three arches, something rural too, in contrast to the same scene today. People wouldn't stand in the middle of the road there now, not for long anyway. Notice how well composed this view is. How wall, fence, road and pavement draw you into the picture.

Taken February 2002 by Jim Halsall. Now the scene is definitely suburban. Kentmere Drive is on the left, with a modern phone box on the corner. Property stands on the right where the embankment was and the built-up area clearly extends beyond the arches.

This is Preston Old Road just before York Terrace looking towards the Feilden Arms and the junction with Livesey Branch Road. Not many years previously trees had lined both sides of the road. The houses on the left and the Mission Hall were fairly recent additions. The houses on Park Farm Road occupy the area now. The policeman is a member of the County police force as the shape of his helmet at the top shows. Note the children at play in the background.

Another February 2002 photo by Jim Halsall with Park Farm Road emerging on the left. Just past the garage is the entrance to St Paul's RC Primary School.

CONGREGATIONAL CHURCH & SCHOOL, CHERRY TREE.

FENISCOWLES CHURCH.

Towards the end of the nineteenth century Cherry Tree, though a sizeable village, had no Non-Conformist place of worship. Mill Hill Congregational was the nearest church. The Reverend David Critchley, Pastor of Tockholes Congregational Church and a carpenter at Cherry Tree Mills championed the cause of Non-Conformity in Cherry Tree. In 1885 at a meeting chaired by him the Cherry Tree non-conformists decided to hold services in Cherry Tree Reading Room. These premises were soon found to be inadequate and it was decided to build a church. The Reverend Critchley acted as foreman for the project and the church was opened on Sunday October 2nd 1887.

It was in the 1830s that moves to build a church at Feniscowles were first made. William Feilden, MP for Blackburn, donated a site and promised to provide the stone. It was Feilden who laid the foundation stone for Immanuel Church on February 5th 1835. A procession almost a mile long travelled from Blackburn to the site. The church was consecrated on October 10th 1836 by the Bishop of Chester. The first incumbent was the Reverend Duncan Campbell. By the time this photograph was taken the Reverend J Grimshaw was installed. The church is a grade two listed building.

The first recorded Annual General Meeting of Pleasington Golf Club was on the 12th March 1892 and the first clubhouse was in Brownlow Terrace. The design for the new clubhouse, to be built in Pleasington Road, was approved in September 1909 and work began on November 11th of that year. The builders were Messrs J Fecitt and Sons.

This photograph was probably taken not long after the clubhouse was opened on 9th June 1910. After the opening ceremony, an exhibition match was played by four professionals. By 1920 it was clear the clubhouse was too small and meetings were held to consider alterations. In 1928 a new ladies' pavilion was opened.

It was in 1844 that the Act for the Blackburn & Preston Railway was passed. The line crossed the Ribble via the line from Wigan. The contract was divided into two sections: Farington to Hoghton, and Hoghton to Blackburn. Most of the difficulties from an engineering point of view were in the latter section, where the River Darwen had to be crossed twice: at Hoghton Bottoms and at Pleasington, where a wooden viaduct was constructed, replaced in1865 by a stone bridge. There were four stations on the line: Bamber Bridge, Farington, Hoghton and Pleasington. The line was opened for passenger traffic on June 1st 1846. The photo was taken from Pleasington Road looking towards Preston with Brownlands Bridge in the distance. By the time Shaw took this photo, the original East Lancashire Railway Company had become part of the Lancashire and Yorkshire Railway.

A VIEW IN PLEASINGTON.

This is the view down Pleasington Road towards the point where it crosses the River Darwen. The building at the bottom is the lodge at the entrance to Feniscowles Hall. The hall was built in 1808 by the Feilden family, who left in 1880, driven out by the stink of the River Darwen which passed almost under their windows. In 1903 the house was put up for auction, but failed to find a buyer. For a while it catered for day trippers and wedding parties, but fell into disrepair during the 1930s. Here an old man is ambling along peacefully with his cow, not a scene you'd expect to come across today.

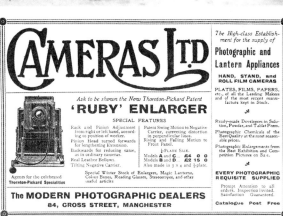

This is the church of St Mary and St John the Baptist, popularly known as Pleasington Priory for its evocation of a medieval past. The tradition is that John Francis Butler of Pleasington Hall had an accident on the site of the Priory and built the church in thanksgiving for his survival. The foundation stone was laid on June 6th 1816 and the church opened on 24th August 1819. The architect was John Palmer and he drew on many architectural traditions in his design, from early English to Regency Gothic. There's a pleasant summer's atmosphere about this scene and one can imagine the worshippers flocking along the dusty lane, making way for the carriages of the well-to-do.

This is the bottom of Preston New Road with St George's Presbyterian Church on the right. The foundation stone was laid on March 4th 1865 by the Rev Francis Skinner. The church opened on June 15th 1868. The Rev A. B. Grosart succeeded Rev Skinner. Grosart was a prolific writer on literary and antiquarian subjects with over 400 books to his name. The last service was held in the church in January 1974 and the building was demolished later that year.

14

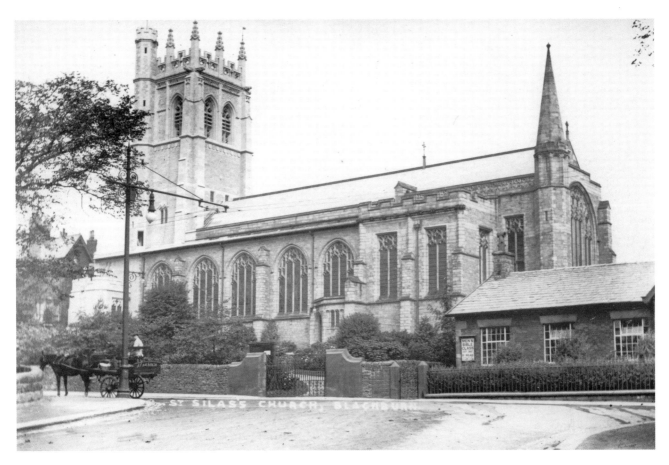

The foundation stone for St Silas' on Preston New Road was laid on December 8th 1849 by Mrs Tattersall, widow of the late W. Tattersall who had donated £1000 to the cost of building the church. St Silas' was opened on May 19th 1898 and consecrated on July 18th of that year. The church was designed by Paley and Austin of Lancaster and built of local stone, with Yorkshire stone dressings and Runcorn stone for the interior walls. The 104 foot high tower seen here was added in 1914. The church is a grade B listed building and can accommodate 400 worshippers.

The blow-up shows John Garsden's butcher's cart making deliveries in the area. His shop premises were in Town Hall Street.

REVIDGE RD, BLACKBURN.

The name Revidge probably originates from old English meaning 'rough edge'. As a thoroughfare it predates even that, as the Roman road to Ribchester came this way. It was called Revidge Lane before Corporation Park was opened in 1857 and there were few houses there. By the time this photograph was taken, around 1910, there were houses all along its length and it was popular with middle class professionals; school teachers, accountants and journalists living there, as well as managers, shopkeepers and salesman. This was taken from near the bottom of Revidge, with Lowood Place on the left and the West View pub on the right beyond the trees.

PRESTON NEW RD, BLACKBURN. №94

At what time of day did Shaw take his photographs? He probably took great pains to make sure his views were traffic free. How many times must he have waited for a tram to pass before clicking his shutter? How much would we give now to have photographs of just those trams?

You'd have to get up early on a Sunday morning now to see Preston New Road looking so tranquil, but as the close-up reveals, this is no Sunday morning view: a good selection of motorised and horse drawn vehicles are on the road. This view was taken near the junction with Lancaster Place, looking towards Preston.

The close-up shows a horse and trap with liveried driver taking some wealthy resident back to his Preston New Road villa. As the motor cars have a number plate, we know that the photo was taken after 1904.

Montague St. was Blackburn's first Baptist church. In 1891 it was proposed that a second church be built. A site was chosen on Leamington Rd and the foundation stone was laid on Easter Sunday 1893. Work was delayed by a building strike and it wasn't until 2nd May 1895 that the official opening was held. Here we see its imposing frontage. The Rev. Walter Mursell was the first pastor. He launched an organ fund which raised £600, and it was installed in January 1897. By the time this photograph was taken the Rev Henry Cook from Glasgow was pastor. It was he who started the church magazine 'The Messenger'.

Leamington Road, formerly Leamington St, was once the home of Blackburn Rovers. There was a grandstand and refreshment pavilion and they played Blackburn Olympic there on 15th October 1881. England played international matches on the ground against Wales and Scotland. Rovers remained there for 9 years before moving to Ewood in 1890. By the time this photo was taken Leamington Road had become a pleasant suburban street popular with business men and skilled tradesmen.

The close-up shows a cart laden with milk kits. People used to come out with their jugs to have them filled. The milk came from cows on a local farm and may well have been delivered by the farmer himself.

NEW RD, BLACKBURN.

The church in this shot is Trinity Methodists at the corner of Montague St and Preston New Rd. It was built in 1879 to the design of draughtsman and book illustrator Herbert W Railton (1857 - 1910). Railton trained with Blackburn architect W S Varley and was a pupil of Blackburn artist Charles Haworth. He lived at 'Brownlow House', Pleasington until leaving to pursue a career as an artist in London in 1885. He achieved national importance as a book illustrator. Trinity merged with Paradise Church and closed in January 1964. The foundations can still be seen below the garage on Preston New Rd.

An open topped tram is returning to the Boulevard. Its route via Richmond Terrace and Ainsworth St differed from the outward journey which went along Church St, Victoria St, Town Hall St and King William St.

Note the centre-of-road tram standard, (these were used to hold the overhead wires in place) unique to Preston New Road.

Gorse Rd from Billinge Avenue. Although some of the houses had been there before, Gorse Rd itself had not been there long when these shots were taken.

These comfortable and imposing villas were home to some of the town's most prominent citizens. George Higson, head of Higson Bros, cotton manufacturers lived at 'Brookfield', Charles Dixon, managing director of the Albert Mill Co lived at 'Royle'. Thomas Parkinson JP, formerly of Blackburn Savings Bank lived at 'Wensleydale'. He was 93 when he died in 1937. Perhaps best known of all was Thomas Boys Lewis who lived at 'Edenholme'. He went to Eton and Oxford, but returned home to manage Springfield Mills. He was a scholar and philanthropist who established the town's textile museum which bears his name.

The house sale sign was put up by estate agent Thomas Sharples, whose office was in Regent St. The old fashioned baby carriage was called a 'basinette', also a 'perambulator', now shortened to 'pram'.

When this was taken the Billinge area was beginning to develop into one of the most desirable residential areas of the town. The houses in Billinge Avenue were built around 1906 of local brick rather than stone and by the time Shaw was setting up his tripod were occupied by solidly middle-class people. George Dymock, who founded the 'People's Mission' in King St, which opened in 1910, lived at 'Edendale', Thomas James Forrest of Forrest Bros. Cotton Spinners lived at 'Forwell' and at 'Bardon' lived Thomas P Ritzema, son of the Thomas Ritzema who was proprietor of the **Northern Daily Telegraph** and who lived nearby at 'Quarry Glen'.

'Billinge' is a name shared with a township near Wigan. It means 'prominent hill'. Blackburn's hill is 807 feet above sea level.

BILLINGE AVENUE, BLACKBURN.

GRANVILLE RD, BLACKBURN.   Nº 110

Another well proportioned thoroughfare of comfortable middle class homes. When this photograph was taken in 1909 Granville Road could boast 7 travelling salesman, 5 clerks, 2 boot makers, a joiner, a plumber, a cabinet maker, a school master, a journalist, a school attendance officer, as well as a number of shopkeepers. In 21 of the 87 properties the head of the household was female.

NEW BANK Rᵈ, BLACKBURN

A lovely shot of New Bank Road without a car in sight. We don't often get the chance today to appreciate the handsome proportions of our streets. The girls on the right are taking an interest in Shaw's camera work.

The close up picks up some of the activity centred around New bank Road's shops. There were two butchers: Riley's and Wrathall's; two fish dealers: Riding's and Walmseley's; Leaver's hardware shop; Billington's drapers; McMyn's chemists and Hayhurst's the tripe dealers. Note the newspaper billboard advertising the ***Daily Mail's*** *'Battle Stories of British Soldiers'*, also the adverts for Rajah Cigars and Capstan Navy Cut Tobacco. A further sign advertises taxis and landaulettes.

CROSS HILL RD, BLACKBURN.

Cross Hill Road running from Preston New Road to Manor Road was a tree lined approach to Cross Hill House back in the 1890s. By the time of the First World War it was lined with substantial villas, homes to people like insurance agent B W Marsden, who lived at 'Oakenhurst'; veterinary surgeon Henry Holroyd, who lived at 'Ballure'; jeweller and diamond merchant George Ainsworth, who lived at 'Troyville' and the manager of the Manchester and County Bank, William Carmichael, who lived at 'Hillrise'.

The young trees planted on either side of the road are protected by cages. They give the road something of a 'garden town' atmosphere, which was sought after by architects and residents.

This is Mavis Road off Buncer Lane, taken just before the First World War. The first of these villa-type, brick-built residences were ready for occupation by 1905. They were popular with the town's successful middle classes. Commercial travellers Fred Hindle and Thomas Dickinson lived there, as did estate agent William Howard. Oil merchant Edgar Ashworth had a house there as did Thomas Mercer of the 'Cherry Tree Machine Company'. Harold Ryden of Ryden Mill Stores lived there. Later in life he moved to Wilpshire and became Chairman of the Blackburn Rural District Council. Richard Ashton, the town's librarian, lived at 'Estcourt'. He was appointed assistant in 1880 and became chief in 1889 on the death of Mr Geddes, remaining in the post until 1937, when he retired after 57 years service.

MAVIS ROAD, BLACKBURN.

A splendid view of the parish church before it became a cathedral. In the foreground is the statue of Queen Victoria. Eleven feet high and weighing 9 tons, it stands on a 14 foot high base which weighs 30 tons. The statue was created by Sir Bertram Mckenna, who also sculpted the bronze figure on the war memorial in Corporation Park. It was unveiled on 30th September 1905 by Princess Louise, Victoria's fourth daughter. It is estimated that 200,000 people turned out to line the Princess' route.

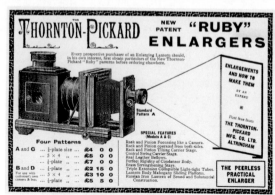

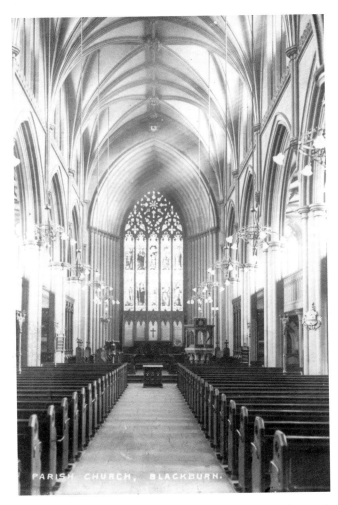

When these shots were taken this was still St Mary's Parish Church. It wasn't until 1926 that the diocese of Blackburn was created and the church elevated to cathedral status. The building had been consecrated 100 years earlier in 1826 though it is believed a church has stood on this site several centuries by then. Its new status meant enlargement and alterations were necessary. Architect W A Forsythe was appointed and in his design the church as seen here was to be the nave of the new cathedral. Work was interrupted by the war and continued until 1968.

The photograph on the left shows the altar. On the right the view is from the altar towards the door.

25

Work began on Corporation Park in February 1855. In August of that year Blackburn contractors Roberts and Walmsley began work on the magnificent entrance gateway and lodge. The park was opened on Thursday on Thursday 22nd October 1857. A crowd of over 60,000 was in attendance. The Mayor William Pilkington of Park Place Mills declared the park open and the crowd were deafened by the roar of the cannon in the battery, trophies from Sebastopol.

It was William Pilkington who donated 3 of the park's 4 fountains. A bandstand was built in 1880. This was demolished and the one in Shaw's photograph was built in 1909. The conservatory was opened in 1900 and the present aviary in 1958. The statue of Flora, who is said to roam the park at night, was installed in 1871.

THE FOUNTAIN, CORPORATION PARK, BLACKBURN.

No 3

CORPORATION PARK, BLACKBURN. No 14.

PHOTOGRAPHER & ARTIST

F. Long

S. PETERS HILL
BLACKBURN

FIRST CLASS
ENLARGEMENTS
CAN BE MADE FROM THIS PHOTO AND
HIGHLY FINISHED IN OIL WATER OR CRAYON
Out door Photography.
ATTENDED TO ON THE SHORTEST NOTICE.

THE NEW BANDSTAND, CORPORATION PARK, BLACKBURN.

"ROYAL VISIT"
BLACKBURN. JULY.10.1913.   N°2

King George V and Queen Mary visited Blackburn on Thursday 10th July 1913. This shot shows the platform erected in front of the town hall where their Majesties were presented to officials and former mayors.

Earlier the Royal Party had visited 'Roe Lee Mill' to see the operatives at work and to inspect an exhibition of goods manufactured at the mill. The operation of a handloom was also demonstrated by Richard and Ellen Ratcliffe.

His Majesty laid the foundation stone for the Public Halls in Northgate.

The King and Queen arrived by motor car and entered Witton Park. They emerged into Buncer Lane, thence along Billinge Avenue, Preston New Road, Granville Road and into Corporation Park.

This photo shows the Broad Walk which was reserved for children over 8 years of age. Each child was given a souvenir flag. As the Royal car passed the children sang the National Anthem, then gave three cheers.

Those living on the route of the procession or within sight of it were granted free gas and electricity for any decorative illuminations from 8.00 in the evening until midnight.

"ROYAL VISIT"
BLACKBURN. JULY.10.1913.   N°1

This is St John's Church in Richmond Terrace built in 1788 by subscription. Henry Sudell of Woodfold paid half the cost. It was originally intended as a chapel of ease to the parish church. The principal architectural feature is the tower, but this wasn't added until 1802. Many of the town's leading merchants and manufacturers are buried in the churchyard. It closed as a church in 1975 and was bought by Blackburn Council who renovated it for use by community groups

St JOHNS CHURCH, BLACKBURN.   No 86

TALBOT & EAMER,

Bona-fide Manufacturers, and Wholesale and Retail Dealers in all

Photographic & Scientific Instruments,

RICHMOND WORKS,
AINSWORTH ST., BLACKBURN (LANCS.)

All kinds of Scientific Wood or Metal Work undertaken.

All Goods advertised in the 'British Journal Almanac' by other Makers may be obtained direct through us at the very lowest possible prices.

SECOND-HAND CAMERAS BOUGHT, SOLD, OR EXCHANGED.

Telegraphic Address :—'EAMER, BLACKBURN.'

A. E. Shaw,
BLACKBURN, LANCASHIRE,

Wholesale Dealer & Publisher of

Pictorial . .

. Post Cards.

Series   Contents   Cards.

No adverts relating to the Shaws have survived and perhaps they never used them. The only promotional material known is this envelope in which they distributed their postcards.

King William Street looking up to Sudell Cross. The Cotton Exchange is on the left. The corner stone was laid on March 10th 1863 and it opened for business as a cotton yarn market in 1865. Later it became a lecture hall, where Charles Dickens read from his work. Later still it became a cinema, known successively as the 'Exchange Hall', the 'Majestic', the 'Essoldo' and the 'Classic'.

February 2002, and modern street furniture and trees have made it hard to get a shot from the same point of view as Shaw. Note the increase in the Cotton Exchange's height, probably done when the building was turned into a cinema. Canopies outside shops protected window displays from the sunlight; no need for anything like that today.

THE MARKET PLACE, BLACKBURN.

Nº 6.

The absence of the much loved market hall tower apart, the feel of this scene is very much the same in Jim Halsall's recent photo. Modernisation of exteriors has taken place and in fact is still being carried out, as evidenced by protective barriers on the left.

It was 30th December 1964 and quite a crowd had gathered to witness a sad scene: the demolition of the market hall tower. Half a dozen blows from the wrecking ball and a part of Blackburn's heritage was a heap of dust and rubble.

In Shaw's photograph it's standing tall, a proud companion to the town hall beyond. Blackburn had been a well known market town as far back as the 16th century. The market hall was opened in 1848, with additional facilities in 1872 and the fish market in 1874.

Blackburn received its Charter of Incorporation on August 28th 1851. The foundation stone for the town hall was laid in 1852. It opened four years later in 1856.

Note the ball on the tower. At noon every day this began to rise until at one o'clock it reached the top, descended quickly and a cannon was fired. This was the signal for workers, very few of whom would have a watch, to return to work.

The Old Toll Bar, Brookhouse, Blackburn.

This is the old toll bar at the junction of Whalley Old Road and Whalley New Road. It was known as the 'Craven Heifer Bar' after the hotel which stood to the left at the corner of Brookhouse Lane. The toll system was introduced in the 18th century to keep the turnpike roads in repair. At its height there were tolls every seven or eight miles. The Local Government Act of 1888 transferred responsibility for roads to the county councils.

The frontage was rebuilt in 1908 to form shop premises and Hartley's Drapers were there for many years. At the rear are cotton warehouses. The building was demolished in 1928. Dunderdale and Yates' Garage, the main Austin dealers later occupied the site.

In February 2002, nothing remains from the original photo but the basic road layout. The garage on the left was the Savoy Garage until the early 1990s when it became Perry's.

BROWNHILL, BLACKBURN. Nº 105

There was a time when built-up Blackburn extended only as far as Larkhill and there were farms along the line of Whalley New Road. As the town expanded these farms were swallowed up. The cemetery opened in 1857 and Cemetery Mill, later Roe Lee Mill, in 1856/7. Cottages for the workers began to appear along the road. Trams appeared, at first only going as far as the cemetery, but in 1902 the route was electrified and extended to the borough boundary at Wilpshire. In 1908 the road near Brownhill was widened. Unemployed textile workers were used to build the fence and paths and in 1909 the railway granted land for tree planting.

The close-up gives a good view of the stately, but cumbersome perambulators that were then in use and the cast iron seating provided by the Corporation.

33

WHALLEY NEW ROAD, BLACKBURN.   Nº 102

Another tranquil view of Whalley New Road, emphasising yet again how attractive our roads and streets were before the advent of the motor car. We're looking towards town here and if we go a little further into the picture, the scene undergoes something of a transformation.

Now we can see that there's a lot more going on than is at first apparent. There are a couple of horse drawn vehicles and an early lorry on the road, as well as the cyclist who seems to be taking an interest in Shaw's work. There are quite a few people on the pavement as well, notably the lady with the child who also seems fascinated by the camera.

In Jim Halsall's recent photo, the iron bench, the railings and the gas lamp have gone, but otherwise the scene is nearly identical to its predecessor seen on page 34. There's even a lone cyclist coming towards the camera, though with different headgear: the flat cap has been replaced by the cycle helmet.

This is Whalley New Road looking towards the town centre with the houses formerly known as 'Woodlands' on the left. These were built towards the end of the 19th century. The remaining houses were built later around 1910. The railings were erected when the road was widened in 1908. It is interesting that the street is lit by gas, yet carried electricity for the trams.

BROWNHILL - BLACKBURN

A view of a Wilpshire that is very much a part of the countryside. This is Knowsley Rd looking towards the railway viaduct from Whalley Rd. It's an idyllic scene with two ladies taking a stroll on a Summer's afternoon, not something that could be done with today's traffic.

This is *'Glendene'* in Knowsley Road. The house had not been long built when this photograph was taken. It was the home of Richard Thompson who was a partner in one of the largest cotton firms in the district with mills in Blackburn, Darwen and Clitheroe. Richard died at *'Glendene'* in his 80th year on August 11th 1924. He left over £100,000 in his will. The house still stands today.

36

WILPSHIRE BOTTOMS

Nº6

Wilpshire township was originally united with Dinckley, but had become separate by the end of the seventeenth century. Road and rail links to Clitheroe pass through the township and encouraged its growth as a residential area.

This is Knowsley Rd looking towards Ribchester Rd with the spire of the Wesleyan Church in the distance. The woman mopping her doorstep on the left of the picture, with her traditional housewife's cotton cap, is mopping and 'donkey-stoning' her doorstep and entrance step. She is as proud of her cottage as the housewives in the rather grander houses across the road.

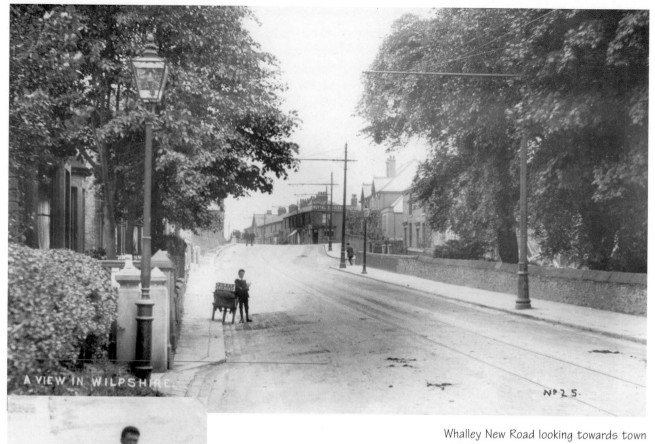

A VIEW IN WILPSHIRE.

Nº 25.

Close-up shows delivery boy leaning on his barrow. Borax was used to remove stains from material. It was sprinkled on then hot water was poured over.

Whalley New Road looking towards town with Ramsgreave Road adjoining from the right and Parsonage Road from the left. The 'Bull's Head', a Thwaites pub, is visible on the right. The 'Rising Sun', owned by Nuttall's, later Lion, then classified as a beerhouse, is just beyond. The 'Rising Sun' was affectionately known as the 'Curran Bun' to its locals. In 1909 Charlie Wilkinson was mine host at the 'Bull's Head', while at the 'Rising Sun' Tom Marsh presided. There is a board on the wall of the 'Rising Sun' giving intresting details of the pub's past.

RISING SUN

The Rising Sun appeared on a list of Blackburn's licensed houses as far back as 1893. Totalling 495 taverns and beer houses, it supported a claim in the London press that Blackburn was "the most beery town in the world". This cosy little pub on the corner of Whalley New Road and Ramsgreave Road was a Nuttall's Little Harwood Brewery ale house and used to affectionately be known as "The Curran Bun" to it's locals. It was frequented by people using the Wilpshire tram lines which last ran in December 1947 and it's tiny "best" room was used by Ramsgreaves Parish Council as their meeting place.

This close-up gives a good view of the 'Bull's Head' and 'Rising Sun'. Note cyclist emerging from Knowsley Road and old gas lamp. Above the door of the 'Bull's Head' is the date it was built - 1907.

In February 2002, Jim Halsall found it difficult to get into precisely the same position as Shaw, who was clearly standing in the road, not the place to be with today's traffic. Little has changed apart from exterior alterations to both public houses.

'The Knolle' in Wilpshire Rd is barely visible for trees now. It was built about 1910 and occupied by John Duckworth, former Liberal MP for Blackburn. He was born at Rishton, the son of George Duckworth, who, with William Eddleston founded the firm of 'Duckworth and Eddleston'. The firm prospered and in 1902 they took over 'Roe Lee Mill', which was visited by King George V and Queen Mary in 1913.

John Duckworth became an MP in 1923. He did not stand in 1929. It is said he took satisfaction in seeing the smoke from the chimneys of Roe Lee Mill from the windows of 'The Knolle'. He died there in 1946 at the age of 82.

Rural Wilpshire again, a panoramic view of a village surrounded by fields. The railway line runs across the foreground and in the distance is the spire of the Wesleyan Church. Today the same view would encompass a sprawl of suburban housing.

Here we are on Ribchester Rd again, now looking the other way over the railway bridge. In the distance is the spire of the recently built Wesleyan Methodist Church. The original chapel was built in 1887, but by 1901 it was clear a bigger church was needed. Morley and Son of Bradford were appointed architects and the corner stone was laid in April 1902. The new church was opened on the 16th of April 1903.

The two horse drawn carts climbing the hill towards Salesbury give the scene a leisurely air.

Did the soldiers of the XXth Valeria Victrix legion march along this road on their way back to the Roman Camp at Ribchester? Did the Scots come this way in 1332 when they burned Ribchester down, or the Earl of Derby's troops when he invaded the Ribble Valley in 1643 during the civil war? Certainly it's a road that leads us back in time. At first glance the scene might seem very much as it does today, but let us take a closer look. Let us walk a little way down this road and see what it has to show us.

Go as far as the railway bridge and we see two elegantly dressed Edwardian ladies approaching. By the time of the First World War Wilpshire had become a desirable place to live. Its population quadrupled between 1871 and 1911. Perhaps the ladies are on their way to take tea in one of the many handsome villas that had sprung up. They are being observed from his ladder by a chap cleaning windows at the 'Wilpshire Hotel'.

WILPSHIRE

Nº 17

A fine view of the tram terminus at Wilpshire. The tram is set to return to town. The 'Bull's Head' is in the distance. After the First World War traffic was on the increase and in 1926 the terminus was moved to the kerbside at the right of this picture. In the background behind the tram can be seen the old smithy at the corner of Parsonage Road, which survived until the 1950s.

Today, some refurbishment of house frontages is in evidence. The layby on the right shows where the tram terminus was. In many ways time has stood still.

A tranquil scene by the 'Wilpshire Hotel' at the junction of Whalley New Rd and Ribchester Rd. No traffic lights were needed in those days. Robert William Hartley was the landlord when this was taken around 1910. He'd been there since the turn of the century. Before him was Ronald Fort and before him John Peel. By the First World War, Robert Hartley had been succeeded by Henry Hoyle.

The Best Soap Made.

For all Domestic Purposes
Dr. Lovelace's Soap
is the Best   Use proves its worth.

For all Household Purposes.

—— USE ONLY ——

DR. LOVELACE'S SOAP

For Snow-white Clothes.   For Good Complexions.

It is made from the finest and purest materials.

Tablets *and* Bars. Original 16 oz. NOT 12 oz. *Note.*

Manufactured by the
EAST LANCASHIRE SOAP CO., LTD., ACCRINGTON.

SOLD EVERYWHERE.

Pure, Economical Reliable.

Perfumed with floral extract.

WILPSHIRE POST OFFICE.   Nº 19

This is a shot of the post office at 'Spring Bank' at the junction with Hollowhead Lane on Whalley Rd. Richard Fowler was postmaster there for many years up until the 1930s when the post office moved to 'Park Villas' in Ribchester Rd, where Jim Stott was postmaster. After the war it moved again to 'Berwyn' in Whalley Rd, where Ronald Warren ran it in conjunction with his newsagents. The telegraph apparatus above the door shows that it would be possible to send telegrams from here.

THE R^Y STATION, WILPSHIRE. No. 23.

The Blackburn, Clitheroe & North Western Junction Railway was formed in 1846. It was intended to build a line from Blackburn to Clitheroe and then to Long Preston to meet the North Western Railway. The first sod was cut at Clitheroe on 30 December 1846. Billington Embankment beyond Wilpshire caused problems with subsidence. Crossing the Calder was the next problem. This required a series of arches, 48 spans in all which took 3 years and 7 million bricks, which were made by George Clarke & Sons of Rishton, to build. The line was opened in 1850.

The station at Wilpshire was opened on 22nd June 1850 and changed its name to 'Wilpshire for Ribchester' in 1874. It closed in September 1962 by which time it was known as 'Ribchester Station', though anyone alighting there might find the walk to Ribchester daunting. A new station, 'Ramsgreave and Wilpshire', opened at the rear of the 'Bull's Head' in 1995.

The foundation stone for Blackburn Orphanage was laid on August 31st 1889 by Alderman John Rutherford JP. The architects Briggs and Wolstenholme designed the building which provided accommodation for 30 boys and 15 girls. The building was opened on July 23rd 1891 by Miss Derbyshire who had made generous contributions to the building fund.

It was James Dixon, a Scot, who came to Blackburn at the beginning of the 1890s, whose hardwork and vision brought the orphanage into existence. He was a superintendent of the Ragged School and worked for the welfare of young children until his death in 1936.

The full story of Dixon and the Orphanage is told in *'The Blackburn Samaritan'* by Trevor Moore.

THE ORPHANAGES, WILPSHIRE. No. 13.

Today Salesbury has been encroached upon somewhat by suburban sprawl. Captured here by Shaw, it is clearly a rural community. In the foreground, seen to better effect in the close up, is Salesbury post office. Proprietor John Smith sold everything from fruit and soap, to cocoa and lamp oil, with no doubt the latest gossip thrown in for good measure. They also sold *Dr. Lovelace's* famous floating soap (see advert on page 43), made in Clayton-le-Moors near Accrington. The quality of Shaw's work is brought home by a further blow-up showing a horse-drawn delivery of American lamp oil to the *'Bonny Inn'*. It was a heavy load needing two horses to draw it. The pub is still owned by Thwaites' Brewery.

SALESBURY CHURCH.   Nº 30

The old church at Salesbury was consecrated in 1807. By 1848 it was condemned as *'ill-built and ruinous'*. It survived for another 40 years.

The foundation stone for St. Peter's shown here was laid on May 8th 1886 and the church was opened in June 1887. It accommodated 300 worshippers. It is an attractive building and its ivy covered walls and sensitive dimensions are well suited to its situation at the edge of the common.

About the time this photograph was taken the incumbent was the Rev Peter Hopwood Hart. The population of Salesbury in 1901 was 217. A century later it was 5,500.

'Talbot & Eamer' were established about 1884 in Blackburn. One of the first cameras they made was the *'Talmer Hand Camera'* with a bag changer. Their *'Flexet Reflector Camera'* shown here was in the shops in 1903. The Shaws would be familiar with their products.

LOVELY HALL, SALESBURY.

The name says it all! This picturesque old house dates from the 16th century. Records show a house on the site in 1246, although the house as seen in the picture was not completed until 1530. It was modified in 1735 and 1874. There is evidence of Tudor, Stuart, Georgian and Victorian influences. It was owned by the Boltons, the Parkers, and then the Starkies of Huntroyde. The land around Lovely Hall is still owned by the Huntroyd estate. Colonel Starkie who lived there in the 19th century had many alterations made.

There's an amusing story from the time of the Colonel's occupancy. He gave a suit of new clothes to one of the villagers, a man known as 'Billy Balshaw', on the latter's 100th birthday. Later the Colonel saw him wearing his usual shabby clothes. *"Why aren't you wearing the new clothes I gave you?"* he demanded. *"A 'wm afeard o'wearin' 'em out,"* the old man replied.

Around the time this photograph was taken the house was leased to Albert Higham, who redesigned the garden, planting a rockery of alpine flowers and installing electricity in the hall itself. During the Second World War the hall was used as a police and civil defence training school.

When William Pilkington of *'Wilpshire Grange'* became mayor in 1857, he launched a building fund for the Infirmary, contributing £2000 of his own money. The foundation stone was laid on Whit Monday 1858 and large crowds lined the route to the Infirmary site to watch the procession from the town centre. Work on the building was halted in 1861 by the cotton famine, but it was sufficiently advanced for it to be used by the Blackburn Relief Fund Committee and work was found for the unemployed in the grounds of the hospital. Work recommenced in 1864 and the hospital opened in 1865. The new *'Victoria Wing'* was opened in 1901 and further extensions made in 1908. *'Royal'* was added to the Infirmary's title in 1914 by King George V.